Ministerially Speaking

Kdp.Amazon Publishing

ISBN 9798676629274

September 2020

By

Robert Beike

A collection of observations,
counsel, witticisms, and warnings...

for what it's worth.

rbeike@aol.com

Table of Contents

Introduction

"How blessed is the man who finds wisdom, and the man who gains understanding…" (Proverbs 3:13 NASB). I have been greatly blessed by others in my pursuit of wisdom and understanding—especially ministerially speaking.

It doesn't seem that long ago—a freshly minted seminary graduate planting a church in Texas, then serving as an associate pastor responsible for education and youth ministrics in Ohio, only to become lead pastor two years later. Yet, nearly four decades of ministry are in my rear-view mirror as I now attempt to help steer other churches into a challenging future in my current regional/associational ministry.

All along the way I have been blessed with friends, colleagues, peers, mentors, and yes, even tormentors to help guide me into wisdom and understanding. They have cautioned and encouraged me, cheered and admonished me, counseled and advised me, and at times, challenged and chastised me. I will be forever grateful.

Many of these guides and mentors sit on my bookshelves in bound volumes, their counsel readily accessible, easily in reach. Others sat in my office or across from me at a restaurant or coffee shop, speaking words of counsel and ministerial wisdom, in person, either informally or quite intentionally. Still others sat in my congregation as former pastors. Two of those need special mentioning. W.A. Fox and Rodney DeLoach were my predecessors with over fifty years of pastoral experience between them. Both remained in the church for a time after stepping down, not as tormentors, but as confidantes, counselors, and ready encouragers. This, I discovered is a rare blessing. Plus, more than a few mentors offered their knowledge from conference platforms to a room full of wisdom seekers like me.

Then, there is one memorable occasion of sitting with Dr. Adrian Rogers in his office/conference room at Belleview Baptist Church in Memphis, Tennessee. This great man of God and princely preacher graciously gave of his time to a handful of Ohio pastors who had traveled to Tennessee for the privilege of soaking up any wisdom and understanding we could. I wish I had been a better sponge.

This ministerial journey would be so much more difficult and hazardous without the collective wisdom of others. In fact, it's likely I wouldn't be looking back on nearly forty years of ministry without them.

I have served in numerous capacities of church ministry—custodian, Sunday School teacher, men's ministry, athletics, deacon, church planter, associate pastor, lead pastor, associational/regional director/strategist, church planting catalyst, and church health consultant. At every step, in each phase of ministry I sought wisdom, advice, and counsel. I still do. But I am now faced with a dilemma. What do I do with all the accumulated knowledge? I have a reservoir of my own "wisdom" that continues to grow. I don't want to reach the edge of eternity hoarding information that may benefit the next generation. Afterall, Christianity is a hand-me-down faith. So I have decided to hand it down in this little book.

This is a book for fellow travelers on the rewarding but hazardous road of ministry. I have sifted through the gravel to find what has been valuable to me. A lifetime of study, observation, research, and experience has been distilled down and delivered in bite-sized chewable bits of ministerial wisdom. For those of my generation, they are like the "Laugh-In" wall where players opened windows, stuck their heads out and delivered comedic one-liners. These, however, are spiritual "one-liners." My hope is that you will find in this book useful stimulus for your own thinking, seeds for sermons and Bible Studies, or a steering mechanism for navigating your own ministry currents.

Here is a collection of my observations, advice, counsel, axioms, witticisms, and warnings… ministerially speaking.

Robert Beike, DMin.

rbeike@aol.com

Discipleship/Body Life

1 God does Altarations.

2 To work effectively for God, walk faithfully with God.

3 Wearing a cross around your neck is not the same as living a cross-centered life.

4 Authentic worship is the heartbeat of a Christian and prayer is their lifeblood.

5 A time of worship should never be the bland leading the bland.

6 What Christians hold in common form an uncommon bond stronger than even biological ties.

7 There is a vital connection between believing God's word and singing God's praise.

8 The church gathers to fuel the church scattered.

9 The Holy Spirit supplies every believer with a healthy appetite for the things of God. It's the church's responsibility to provide them with a healthy diet.

10 The extent of a church's ministry will not exceed the depth of its members' devotion.

#11 The Maturation of a Christian is a spiritual construction project overseen by the Holy Spirit and assisted by other Christians, who are also under construction.

#12 Making fully devoted followers of Christ is not a motto, it's a mandate.

#13 Unless your worldview is filtered through the Bible, your only grid for decision making is the world's view.

#14 Without roots grounded deep in scripture there can be no spiritual fruit.

#15 When it comes to being disciples, Jesus expects us to get it together.

#16 Christianity is fleshed out through authentic human relationships,

#17 Christianity is a hand-me-down-faith.

#18 We most resemble Christ when we are generous.

#19 All of life is a stewardship. As trustees, Christians are to maximize for good the goods they've been given.

#20 Generosity is not measured in amounts but attitudes.

#21 Being born-again spiritually is like being parachute dropped behind enemy lines. Christians are on mission and targets of the enemy.

#22 To finish strong, avoid haziness, laziness, and craziness.

#23 Humans are created for community and hard-wired for relationships.

#24 Being imitators of Christ often means ministering at a "gut-level" point of need.

#25 Disciples take shape in community.

#26 Making disciples is more caught than taught.

#27 We all need cheers from our peers.

#28 True worship is a loving act by a redeemed people toward a loving God.

#29 True worship is an appropriate spiritual response to the self-revelation of God.

#30 God-honoring worship is sincere, Spirit-led, Christ-focused, and scripture-based.

#31 Worship is not a spectator sport or a form of entertainment.

#32 Worship magnifies the Lord, unifies the church, and edifies believers.

#33 Multiplication is to take place at every level of the mission of God.

#34 Generosity should be an everyday activity of Christians animated by the Spirit of God and motivated by the love of others.

#35 Faith is the spiritually rich atmosphere in which Christians live and breathe.

#36 Following Jesus is transformative. It is not a patchwork effort or a harmonizing with the old life.

#37 Following Christ means you are God's representative on earth.

#38 God's gifts do not come with an expiration date.

#39 Faith in God enables you to see beyond the obvious, above the obstacles, and focus on His objectives

#40 Stay plugged into God all week to avoid a cold worship engine on Sunday.

#41 The breastplate of righteousness has two layers. One is foundational from a right standing with God, the other is formational from right living before God.

#42 The belt of truth holds your credibility in place.

#43 We need shoes of peace because we have feet of clay.

#44 Let your worship be God-glorifying, Christ-centered, Spirit-directed, believer-edifying, and guest-appealing.

#45 A believer's level of devotion to Christ is evident in everything from the tone of their voice to how they spend their time.

#46 Some "Christians" are dead and don't know it, and others are alive but don't show it.

#47 Godly giving is:

(1) Graceful
(2) Joyful
(3) Liberal
(4) Supernatural
(5) Willing
(6) Spiritual
(7) Loving
(8) Sacrificial
(9) Sharing
(10)   Daring

#48 Religious legalism is a form of endless trivial pursuit.

#49 Make your life add up to something positive--- count the cross as a plus sign.

#50 Small groups are not small potatoes when it comes to making disciples.

#51 Making disciples requires impactful relationships, individual responsibility, and intentional reproduction.

#52 Faith is a protective shield that both extinguishes the fiery arrows of the enemy and distinguishes a believer from the world.

#53 Wearing a cross is not the same as bearing a cross.

#54 Truth and integrity are to the family what a greenhouse is to flowers.

#55 The responsibility of child rearing is not transferable. Do your part.

#56 Add value to your family. Show them some appreciation.

#57 God has commissioned you as a "home missionary." Lift up Christ at home.

#58 Practice holy amnesia. Choose to "forget" the faults of your family.

#59 Never use your family for a sermon illustration without their permission. They may forgive you, but they won't forget.

#60 Maintain a regular date night with your spouse. Even it is just a walk for ice cream or a drive in the country.

#61 Ministers are not exempt from a day of rest.

#62 Sometimes the most spiritual thing you can do is take a nap.

#63 You can make up many things. But you can't make up time not spent with your family.

#64 Take time regularly to refresh and renew.

Leadership/Church Health

#65 Flake's Formula is not a dandruff shampoo, but it is effective for a healthy Sunday School.

> - Know the possibilities
> - Enlarge the organization
> - Provide space and equipment
> - Enlist and train workers
> - Go after the people

#66 Leaders must be spiritual environmentalists and organizational climatologists if they expect healthy conditions for growth.

#67 Who you are following is a test of lordship. Who is following you is a test of leadership. What follows after you is a test of legacy.

#68 Borrowing another organization's vision is like trying to drive by another car's headlights.

#69 The formula for a toxic church: Fellowship ÷ Factions x Friction = Fractures + Dysfunction.

#70 In Ministry, servant defines who you are and describes what you do.

#71 Pastors do not serve for prestige, profit, position, power, or even personal choice—but because they are hand-picked by a holy God.

#72 God provides the stamina for running the course He lays out for you.

#73 When funding ministry, think "cargo pants" not "skinny jeans."

#74 Change comes slowly to most and almost never to some.

#75 Beware of "whack-a-mole" people in your organization who knock down every new idea.

#76 Some churches are like Peter Pan. They refuse to grow up and prefer living in a kind of "Never, Never Land."

#77 Leading change in an organization is like being in a snake pit. You must keep moving but can't do anything too suddenly.

#78 There is a Dr. Jekyll and Mr. Hyde character to every congregation.

#79 Be faithful in the mundane as well as the momentous.

#80 Minister to both the "Jacob" and "Israel" components of the flock.

#81 Healthy churches provide at least 60 ministry opportunities foe every 100 members.

#82 It is not enough to feed God's people the truth, they must learn to feed themselves.

#83 Develop a strategy and structure for connecting people in authentic relationships.

#84 As a church leader, don't be bashful about asking disciples to give toward ministry--and teach them how.

#85 Vision is part hindsight, part insight, and part foresight.

#86 Anticipate divine appointments.

#87 Unity, not uniformity, is the formula for successful teamwork.

#88 Common focus not conformity leads to victory

#89 "Brothers, what we do in life echoes in eternity." – Maximus (Gladiator)

#90 "Whatever comes out of these gates, our best chance of survival is working together." – Maximus (Gladiator)

#91 Practice a "catch and release" strategy. Help people catch God's vision for the church, then release them for God's mission in the world.

#92 Pastoring a church can be like a walk in the park—Jurassic Park!

#93 Avoid becoming trapped by the familiar, wed to the comfortable, and tricked into fixations and inflexibility.

#94 Without healthy change healthy growth is not possible.

#95 Jesus is the ultimate change agent.

#96 Healthy ministries are not tethered to the past or trapped by the traditional--Neither are they enamored by everything new.

#97 Renewal takes place not where there is a mindset of resistance, but within a spirit of receptivity to God's activity.

#98 Resisting healthy change robs you of God's best.

#99 God wants to do something surprising, amazing, and miraculous in your ministry.

#100 Without an environment conducive to change, status quo will prevail.

#101 Change demands time, patience, persistence, and a plan.

#102 Many churches suffer from abnormal "weather" patterns—cold fronts of tradition that block progress, or storms of conflict and resistance of historical proportions.

#103 To create a climate of change, inject elements of education, inspiration, and experimentation.

#104 For many, change feels like walking off a cliff blindfolded. Unless people are reasonably assured that the landing won't be fatal, they won't take the plunge.

#105 While navigating change, hold tight to fundamental values.

#106 Failures are necessary tuition for a better future.

#107 Don't confuse theology with methodology.

#108 Leverage strengths to facilitate change.

#109 In the change process you may need to leave your comfort zone but never your strength zone.

#110 As with wine and wineskins, the contents of the church's message is vital. The packaging can and should change.

#111 Step one in the change process is acknowledging that God is in charge.

#112 We serve an innovative God. In the beginning He stepped from behind the curtain of nowhere on to the platform of nothing and spoke the worlds into being.

#113 Change is the vehicle. Transformed lives is the goal.

#114 When you become aware of God's intended future for you or your ministry, cost becomes an investment, and sacrifice a love offering to God.

#115 The nature of change is costly, but the nature of not changing is deadly.

#116 Biblical truth is forever. Godly vision and values serve as lasting anchors. But methods and styles have a shelf life.

#117 We may remember former things with fondness and yearn for their return, but we can't reclaim yesterday.

#118 A church cannot afford to just perpetuate traditions or fond memories while the world around it dies and goes to hell.

#119 It is easier to add productive elements to a ministry than try to eliminate entrenched unproductive ones.

#120 Just-in-time training is just what ministry workers need.

#121 Discover, develop, and deploy ministry gifts.

#122 A Christian's speech should be grace-full, hope-full, and help-full.

#123 The end-times may capture our imagination, but the mean-time demands our attention.

#124 Opportunity may knock, but sometimes, it begs. Be aware of the needs around you.

#125 God prepares you to fit into His plans.

#126 Starting a church requires God, energy, knowledge, and money. Start with God!

#127 God's agents are all valuable, but none are irreplaceable.

#128 You may need to wait your turn to lead but you don't need to just sit in the waiting room.

#129 God providentially sets the extent of your ministry. Be intentional about possessing it.

#130 Shepherd with integrity of heart and skillfulness of hand – (Psalm 78:72)

#131 A vision without a plan is just a delusion.

#132 A successful journey requires a far vision and a near look.

#133 There is a time for everything, but there is not time for everything. Prioritize.

#134 Retool your skills and reinvent your style from time to time.

#135 Seeing the "not yet" that will be, and must be, is the first step toward its reality.

#136 A vision is where God wants you to be after you do what God wants you to do.

#137 The human eye has the remarkable capacity to see the light from a candle 10 miles away. But, can you see the flickering light of a world in spiritual need?

#138 A vision requires being in position to receive it, helping partners to believe it, and having a plan to achieve it.

#139 The seed of every God-given vision is a burden on the heart—a concern that causes you to dream of solutions.

#140 A minister labors in God's field, sows God's seed, and reaps God's harvest in God's good time.

#141 The color of your ministry's unique strategy must be determined by the hues and shades of your specific situation.

#142 Strategizing begins with the destination in mind.

#143 Are you a ministry F.I.T. for your community?

F. Familiar with the people who live there? Or

I. Indigenous to the people that live there? Or

T. Willing to spend enough **time** to become one with the people who live there?

#144 Develop a Teflon reputation so negative gossip doesn't stick.

#145 When the Savior is lifted up in your life, others will also be elevated.

#146 As a leader, remember that the same people who make you the object of their affection may one day make you the subject of their defection.

#147 Changed people can change their world.

#148 Pursue excellence. It will lead you to better places.

#149 Never settle for mediocre when God designed you for meteoric.

#150 Don't get too puffed up. Sometimes people indicate a preference for Baptist just because they can't spell Episcopalian.

#151 All ministry is state-of-the-heart.

#152 As you grow older, you can choose to be propped up on a porch in a rocker wearing a "do not disturb" sign, or you can put on running shoes and finish the race with grace.

#153 Choose making God famous over making yourself comfortable.

#154 God wants to stretch you to your full God-given potential. Satan just wants you bent out of shape.

#155 The lion tamer uses a three-legged stool to keep the lion from focusing on one thing. Don't let the enemy distract you from your main purpose in life.

#156 Healthy churches provide healthy—

> - Goals and plans
> - Training and resources
> - Accountability and alignment
> - Support and coaching

#157 A Health-E church consists of healthy—

> - Expectations
> - Equipping
> - Evaluation
> - Encouragement

#158 Entropy is real, but it isn't what it once was.

#159 Beware the shadowy borderline between motivation and manipulation.

#160 Many churches become so hardened by their traditions that any attempt to move them results in large portions breaking away.

#161 There's no point in being pessimistic. It wouldn't work anyway.

#162 Unless a valid alternative reality becomes evident, no change will occur in the current reality.

#163 If you think you are God's gift to the church—you are! God gives gifts to the church by gifting people to serve.

#164 Creativity runs in God's family.

#165 The Church has always existed on the thin edge between expansion and extinction. Innovation is often the tipping point.

#166 The extent of a leader's success is largely due to the depth of their devotion and the breadth of their vision.

#167 Practice Gospel-tality—Christ-centered hospitality.

#168 Christian hospitality puts grace to work.

#169 The moment we see a new church as competition we take our eyes off the harvest.

#170 A "Silo" church protects itself from others. A "Lighthouse" church projects Christ's light to others.

#171 An overly inward focus acts against the outward thrust of the church.

#172 Help God's people identify their role in God's mission.

#173 Share good news...for a change.

#174 Christians have a "show and tell" ministry. Be good news as well as share good news.

#175 Every believer is a missionary. Learn how to live like one.

#176 "Witnessing" may be the great omission of the church.

#177 When it comes to believers participating in God's mission, the Spirit is willing, but the flesh is weak.

#178 Missional living requires developing missional eyesight. Take a fresh unobstructed look at the cities, towns, communities, and neighborhoods around you.

#179 Don't be so focused on the harvest that you forget to plant seeds.

#180 Being imitators of Christ often means ministering at a "gut-level" point of need.

#181 The harvest field is also a battlefield.

#182 Christians adding genuine salt to the world's simmering stew of spiritual ideas could alter the whole flavor for the glory of God.

#183 God's family is designed for the multiplication of missional believers.

#184 God's agenda is greater than His agents.

#185 Empowering by the Holy Spirit provides the great ignition for the great commission.

#186 God's heart and hand works in perfect concert to accomplish His mission.

#187 God is the master architect. He providentially draws lines connecting the people of God with the people who need God.

#188 The great commission has a "flip-side." In addition to the church going into the world, God brings the world to the church.

#189 You can make a world of difference where you are with what you have if you are willing to give it away.

#190 World evangelism is more than a geographical quest ("go into all the world"). It is primarily a peoples quest ("all nations").

#191 Getting the gospel contents out of its human containers and into the world is the work of the Holy Spirit.

#192 Spiritual myopia is a common affliction among churches.

#193 In the beginning, when God said, "Let there be light," He had the end clearly in mind. (Revelation 21:23-24).

#194 The kingdom of God has an open-door policy.

#195 Evangelism and church planting are invasions of the realm of darkness.

#196 The portrait of the church is not to be a still life. It is a motion picture, action adventure.

#197 Don't let your witnessing approach become a reproach to the unsaved.

#198 "Let there be light" is a mission statement.

#199 Don't let worldliness eclipse your Sonlight.

#200 Messing up your life will mess up your gospel message.

#201 You are a personal love letter written by the hand of God and sent into the world for all to read.

> ➢ Be sure of your content.
> ➢ Be careful of your style.
> ➢ Be aware of your circulation.

#202 A Godly presence is the necessary foundation and framework of evangelism.

#203 There is no substitute for "being there." Connect with people where they live, work, and play.

#204 Being missional requires an incarnational, relational, and sacrificial presence.

#205 Flesh out the great commission among others in your sphere of influence.

#206 Proclaim the gospel with cultural sensitivity.

#207 When properly understood, culture offers common ground, and a conduit, for the good news of God's life changing love.

#208 We persuade others because they matter to God.

#209 God's providence is the indispensable key to the process of evangelism.

#210 Trust God to remove scales of spiritual blindness, and ready human hearts for the gospel seed.

#211 Winning the world to Christ is a spiritual enterprise and is possible only when Spirit-filled believers on mission for God learn to trust and obey Him completely.

#212 Compromising with the corrupt will contaminate your witness.

#213 Before a church can be part of turning the world upside down (or right-side up) it first must be turned inside out.

#214 Unless a church's vision becomes viral it will not infect enough of the body to be contagious to the community.

#215 God often wrings
the gospel out of His
people through
suffering.

#216 To see people as
Jesus sees them, ask
God to correct your
spiritually impaired
vision.

#217 Learn to see as
God sees and go as God
goes.

#218 Despite the
failures of God's
people, God hasn't
scrubbed His mission.

Prayer/Spiritual Formation

#219 One person's prayer can be all that separates a person or a people from disaster.

#220 The effectual prayer of a righteous man avails much. So, by all means, teach, model, and practice effectual prayer.

#221 Group prayer adds muscle to the body of Christ.

#222 When we kneel side-by-side and pray face-to-face with God, we work shoulder-to-shoulder for the cause of Christ and stand back-to-back to defend the faith.

#223 Blanket prayer by the church can warm the community to the claims of Christ.

#224 Ask God for His blessings. Seek God's guidance. Knock on Heaven's door for necessary resources.

#225 Spiritual warfare can only be won with spiritual weapons.

#226 Consider deploying a S.W.A.T. (Spiritual Weapons and Tactics) team in your community.

#227 Intensive prayer is the key to unlocking closed minds, opening blind eyes, straightening twisted lives, and liberating bound spirits.

#228 Learn to pray dialogue, not just monologue.

#229 Prayer is the gateway to advancing the kingdom of God.

#230 Prayer emboldens the witness and empowers the witnessing process.

#231 Fervent and faithful prayer reduces strongholds, removes obstacles, and releases those held captive to the enemy.

#232 The impassioned prayers of the righteous are violent invasions of the province of the impossible.

#233 We are in a spiritual battle. Pray to win!

#234 God leans forward when His children pray.

#235 Any place can be a sacred place when it's a place you meet with God.

#236 When prayer "goes viral" in the church you can expect an infection of Godliness in the community.

#237 We never see clearer than when we are on our knees before God.

**#238 Prayer
strengthens us for life's
challenges and
stretches us to
conform to God's
purposes.**

**#239 Through prayer,
our agenda is replaced
by God's agenda, our
opinions defer to His,
and our wills bow to
God's will.**

#240 Prayer is the work of the church and a weapon in the war against wickedness.

#241 Prayer unlocks the door to becoming a great commission church.

<u>Preaching/Teaching</u>

#242 Preaching is delivering a Biblical train of thought intended to move people from where they are to where God wants them to be.

#243 Never assume people are on the same page as you just because they are in the same room as you.

#244 Preachers, sharpen your message like a pencil. Eliminate everything that doesn't contribute to the point.

#245 Some sermons are like dictionaries. The words are interesting and informational, but there is no common theme to link them together.

#246 Preaching is doing grunt work in God's construction business. We carry the bricks He provides to build Godly lives.

#247

 As a preacher/teacher, you spend your life getting a grip on God's word only to discover it was really the other way around.

#248 Sermon application is putting everyday handles on eternal truths.

#249 An arresting sermon introduction will:

> - Explore a relevant issue
> - Orient the audience to the Biblical text
> - Contextualize the issue and text for today
> - Personalize the truth for the audience

#250 A preacher should be a professor in the study, and a pastor, poet, painter, prophet, and persuader in the pulpit.

#251 The path to a God-honoring pulpit begins in the study and passes through the prayer closet—or the other way around.

#252 The outcome of your preaching depends on the input of your study, the output of your praying, and the outpouring of God's Spirit.

#253 Some preachers take a Biblical text and make a beeline to the cross. Others make a beeline to their hobby horse.

#254 Pulpits are the front lines of the war on error and words are the weapons of our warfare.

#255 Sermon application is necessary because of the gap between God's will and Man's ways.

#256 For preachers, words are the currency of communication and personal holiness is the currency of credibility.

#257 You may be inspired by other preachers, encouraged by other people, and equipped by seminary professors, but ultimately you are chosen by God to preach.

**#258 Frame your
sermon title in a way
that is intriguing to
the twenty-first
century mind.**

**#259 Preach a series of
connected messages
when feasible. There is
significance in
sequence.**

**#260 A sermon series
provides an on ramp
for hearers.**

#261 A timely sermon series can address perceived needs and broaden understanding of the Bible.

#262 You can learn a lot about preaching after you have been taught how to preach.

#263 Use sermon outlines to frame truth that transforms.

#264 Sermon outlines give structure and cohesion to a Biblical message.

#265 Outlining your sermon can provide homiletic focus.

#266 A sermon outline can create flow and avoid meandering.

#267 Connect all the main points of a sermon to the one big idea.

#268 Maximize sermon structure by using complete sentences rather than incomplete phrases in your outline.

#269 Contemporize a sermon outline for today's hearers.

#270 Personalize a sermon outline by using second person pronouns.

**#271 Put sermon
outlines to work by
investing in verbs,
employing imperatives,
and infusing
inspiration.**

**#272 Memorable
sermons are clear,
simple, and use
thought provoking
phrases, and
reiteration.**

**#273 Never undervalue
sermon introductions.
Even a thoroughbred
that stumbles out of
the gate has difficulty
catching up.**

#274 Effective sermon introductions create an appetite for the main course.

#275 Sermon introductions must overcome disinterest, distractions, and spiritual distance.

#276 The art of the start of a message is to overcome inertia and apathy in the hearers.

#277 For speakers, gaining attention and interest is not a luxury, but a necessity.

#278 A stimulating introduction is like stirring a pot of chili that has sat for a long time.

#279 An introduction must answer the questions:

> ➢ **Why should I listen?**
> ➢ **Where are you headed?**
> ➢ **What will be the payoff?**

#280 Facilitating a Bible study is like being an air-traffic controller. Allow many views to circle the room, but God's truth must be brought in for a landing.

#281 Verbs, not verbiage, carry the freight in effective sermons.

#282 The challenge of preaching and teaching God's word is to put heavenly concepts into earthly language.

#283 A Biblical sermon is rooted in the original author's intent.

#284 When preaching, be personal—direct and engaging.

#285 Sermons that S.T.I.C.K. are:

<u>S</u>imple and clear

<u>T</u>extually grounded

<u>I</u>ntentionally focused

<u>C</u>ontextually relevant

<u>K</u>inetic with movement and energy.

#286 Preachers are like flies on a screen door. There are some inside a church wanting to get out and some outside wanting to get in.

#287 There is a confederacy of ideas. When one idea surfaces others emerge to keep it company.

#288 Whatever the sermon length, it should be of Biblical proportions.

#289 No matter how carefully a Biblical passage is exegeted, and how skillfully a message is crafted, a sermon will ultimately be judged on its delivery.

#290 People don't care what you know until they know what you know matters to them.

#291 Avoid "Captain Obvious" sermons.

#292 Preach so God's truth is etched on your hearer's hearts and echoes in their minds as they live their lives.

#293 An effective sermon title is a message about the message before the message.

#294 Biblical exegesis is drawing the meaning from the text. Biblical exposition is drawing from the exegesis the meaning for the people.

#295 A preaching event should be more than just a moment in time. It should be a momentous time when lives are changed.

#296 A sermon title can add "curb appeal" to the message.

#297 A pure heart has more power in the pulpit than a polished delivery.

#298 The difference between God-given dreams and man-driven schemes is faith in God.

#299 True happiness is not found in a selfish "designer life" full of designer clothes, a dream home, trophy spouse, and cool friends. True happiness is found in The Divine Designer who fills you with Himself, allowing you to experience the abundant life from the inside out.

#300 If you teach children they are no better than animals, don't be surprised if they act like beasts.

#301 If you feel you can't be useful to God because your ministry resume has too many blanks, let God fill in the blanks.

#302 We receive God's wisdom on the installment plan.

#303 God draws a circle around His own in which we rest. He then draws a line over which the enemy cannot cross.

#304 Humility is tuition for the Lord's school of salvation.

#305 Let God's footsteps be your pathway.

#306 The key to experiencing God's guidance is to patiently wait for it.

#307 In a culture adrift with uncertainty, God's word is a secure anchor.

#308 Even the Lord's special instruments can become unusable due to uncleanness.

#309 The doors of God's house swings both ways; invitations to come and imperatives to go.

#310 God gives you all you need, to do all He wants you to do, for as long as He wants you to do it.

#311 Always remember that God loves you and gave His best for you.

#312 God's call upon your life is upward, fulfilling, and abundant.

#313 Keep your feet on the Rock and your eye on the sky.

#314 A little restraint can keep a lot of riffraff out of your life.

#315 There's courage in the everyday choices of life.

#316 Live with your back to the past, your face to the future, and your feet planted firmly in the present.

#317 God's timing is perfect—our understanding is not.

#318 Every believer has an original divine blueprint.

#319 We are on a "need to know" basis with God.

#320 Life is more rhythmic than random. Get in tune with God.

#321 Be opportunistic. Make the most of your chances as well as your choices.

#322 Obeying God may sometimes lead to adverse circumstances, but it always leads to abundant blessings.

#323 A Christian need not fear dying. Fear, instead, not living up to your God-given potential.

#324 God is doing something in our day that is difficult to believe. It requires us to "look, "observe," and "wonder." (Habakkuk 1:5)

#325 God, who helped in the past, is your hope in the present.

#326 God is always the same, but He doesn't always respond the same way.

#327 God will always act the right way on your behalf, but maybe not right away.

#328 God made Man with a handful of dust but gave him a heartful of deity.

#329 The God of your emergency needs is also the God of your everyday needs.

#330 With God, we can live in heavenly peace, even when all hell breaks loose.

#331 Be an "all of my days" seeker of God.

#332 If you don't deal with guilt, it will deal you a bad hand.

#333 The Lord of Heaven is also Lord of History.

#334 God smiles on us even when circumstances frown on us.

#335 If you're wrestling with discouragement, rest in God.

#336 When you are singing the blues God can change your tune.

#337 Don't be shocked by the ungrounded hatred of those desiring to short-circuit the glory of God.

#338 God will forgive you only when He's good and ready. Thankfully, He's both good and ready.

#339 In the University of Adversity, make your textbook the "good book."

#340 Prize wisdom and wisdom will surprise you.

#341 Pursue wisdom and wisdom will preserve you.

#342 Goodness, like health, is not contagious. Yet, we are easily infected by iniquity.

#343 When you meet temptation, make a right turn, and keep going straight.

#344 God's word is our owner's manual. Refer to it often. Adhere to it faithfully.

#345 The steps of a good man are ordered by the Lord. So are his starts and stops.

#346 Experiences, like appetites, keep coming. What you do with them helps determine your future.

#347 When counting your blessings, you sometimes discover some blessings count more than others.

#348 All honest labor is honorable. But, honestly, I want to believe my labor makes a difference.

#349 Fake news is as old as the Garden of Eden—and it remains just as sinister and destructive.

#350 Who is the biggest liar in your town? Hint—the devil!

#351 Sharing untruths make us dummies in Satan's ventriloquism act.

**#352 Lies are Satan's
native tongue. It
should remain
unknown to us.**

**#353 Fish bite not
because of the bait, but
because they are
hungry. We all have an
appetite for sin that
needs to be curbed.**

**#354 Guard your mind.
Poisonous thoughts
lead to ruinous habits.**

**#355 In God we trust—
for life, liberty, and the
pursuit of holiness.**

**#356 If you want to
count for God, don't
count on your own
"goodness."**

**#357 Wisdom's rewards
are out of this world—
long life, riches, honor,
pleasantness, peace,
and happiness.**

#358 Mercy and truth are opposites that attract favor and esteem.

#359 Bad people twist good words.

#360 When others turn against you, turn to God.

#361 Roadblocks can become building blocks and not stumbling blocks when you build your life on the cornerstone.

#362 At the heart of idolatry is a heart at odds with God.

#363 Strive to be your best so you can help others be their best.

#364 We are all part of God's beautiful tapestry, but we may pass from the scene before the eternal picture is complete.

#365 Grab hold of Godly wisdom and hold on for dear life.

www.ingramcontent.com/pod-product-compliance
Lightning Source LLC
Chambersburg PA
CBHW020550160726
47991CB00002B/672